TENDING the MASTER'S GARDEN

Joyful Thanksgiving for the Beauty of God's Handiwork

Paintings by
Charles Peer

Writings by
May Harris Gray

TENDING *the* MASTER'S GARDEN

Joyful Thanksgiving for the Beauty of God's Handiwork

New Leaf Press

First Printing: April 1996

Copyright ©1995 by New Leaf Press. All rights reserved. Printed in the United States of America. No part of this book may be used or reproduced in any manner whatsoever without written permission of the publisher, except in the case of brief quotations in articles and reviews. For information write: New Leaf Press, Inc., P.O. Box 726, Green Forest, AR 72638.

ISBN: 0-89221-315-9
Library of Congress Catalog: 95-73126

Unless otherwise noted, all Scripture quotations are from the New King James Version of the Bible.

Dedications:

To my family
... how good ... ... near and far. — May Harris Gray
... staircase of Palmstr. 17, ...
...ad a couple of rabbits at/on the Lage...
little Schreibergarden/similar to victory garden the
even spent the whole weekends there - that's where my mom's Peer
jar the white chlorine powder or similar disinfectant and
pulled, I tripped, fell, and cut my forehead open in the
on Feldstrasse around the corner from Paradiesstr. facing
angry and my mom had to clean it up before she was able to
out and was bleeding very much from my forehead over my r:
still have 3/4" scar there). There I rode with the bicycle
leftover/missed grain. My mother then had /took care of hission to reprint certain poems in the
Diminiumsacker, there I always found something (E: mom mea

Also to Charles N. Boehms, Dean of Academic Affairs of Georgetown College, Georgetown, Kentucky,
for permission to reprint an article in their publication, *Kentucky In American Letters, Vol. III.*

"Garden of the Lord" written by request of the Van Buren, Arkansas, Garden Gate Garden Club, 1971.
— May Harris Gray

I would like to express my appreciation to Bill and Dede Hutcheson for the inspiration that began this
project; to Dave Andrus for his continuing encouragement, advise, and aesthetic judgement; and also to my
supportive family and dear friends. I would like to acknowledge the owners of paintings included in this
book whose names appear on the final page.
— Charles Peer

And the Lord God planted a garden eastward in Eden (Gen. 2:8).

The Garden of the Lord

For the Lord will comfort Zion . . . and He will make her wilderness like Eden, and her desert like the Garden of the Lord (Isa. 51:2).

God made the first garden and only His hand
Commands the rain and sun
That quickens the seed, the heart of the flower,
Only His will is done.

Thus we rejoice in the green of the year;
Offer thanks in the golden glow;
Sing praises when the bough is white
With soft, new-fallen snow.

In a garden we touch the hem of His robe;
In a garden we make our prayer;
We can open the gate, whatever the season,
And walk with the Master there.

Spring Song

The blossoms on this April day
Seem to breathe the breath of love
In cadences of loveliness
Where leaf-sweet shadows move.

The voice of love is everywhere
Deep-rooted in the mothering earth,
The glory of the resurrection,
New beauty and new birth.

Everywhere the touch of love,
Of beauty in the quickening sod;
For beauty's other name is Truth,
Love's other name is God.

*For as the earth bringeth
forth her bud, and as
the garden causeth the things that
are sown in it to spring forth;
so the Lord God will cause
righteousness and praise to spring
forth before the nations* (Isa. 61:11).

Another Spring

Still longing for
A warmer sun that speaks to me,
A softer wind that sings to me,
My windows opened to the sky today.
Underneath the frozen sea of glass
Something has crumbled shards of ice and clay;
Something invisible,
Something without an end, and suddenly
The hillside and the valleys
Are in bloom.

This is the way
It was that other spring
When life was young and softer winds
Measured the hours, and I remember the turn
In the road
Cool in the shadows, the silence
In the hills around, the beauty
And the song.

Now unto the King eternal, immortal, invisible, the only wise God, be honor and glory for ever and ever. Amen (1 Tim. 1:17).

CPEER

Although the house is old and forsaken, the flowers and vines still bloom year after year. The birds, the wildlife, and the wayward winds scatter the seed far beyond the borders of a place that was once called home.

Thinking of this sweet place of peace we are reminded that the God of mercy, self-sacrifice, and love plants in the hearts of His people His virtues and ideals.

When spring lays a carpet of green and gold in the early light of dawn, and blossoms are shining like the stars above, it is easy to forget that all of Eden was lost.

O Lord our Lord, how excellent is thy name in all the earth! who hast set thy glory above the heavens (Ps. 8:1).

When Small Things Rest

There is a moment when the dark comes down
When small things turn like blossoms interlaced
To their own place of rest, a crown
Of leaves; and sweetly rising I have traced
The echo of a thin, low song between
The quickly blurring petals of a bloom.
And yet a part of day can still be seen
In moth-white wings outside my lamp-lit room.

Within the mystery of the twilight hour
It seems that time itself has paused to rest.
No scythe to crush the smallest home-grown flower,
No wind to rock the little wild bird's nest.
This is the homing hour, the moment when
The peace of twilight tucks our small ones in.

This New Hour

Even the wind is singing tonight.

The bells peal out as though

To reach the very crest of heaven

Hidden by clouds of snow.

I never thought I would look upon

A sky so pure and white;

A world so beautiful it seems

The gift of second sight.

Surely this bright new hour speaks

A message of good will —

Love, peace, and a better hope,

The earth a garden still.

The Lord lift up his countenance upon thee, and give thee peace (Num. 6:26).

Sky Lines

(Over the Blue Aegean Sea)

Light,
And the sky is bending,
Bending near and new —
Almost as if my hand could reach
And touch the blue.

Night,
And the nearness still
Falls close upon the land —
Almost as if a star could lean
And touch my hand.

This is the day which the Lord hath made; we will rejoice and be glad in it (Ps. 118:24).

Beloved, let us love one another:
for love is of God; and every one
that loveth is born of God,
and knoweth God
(1 John 4:7).

In Love with Life

Shadow and sun . . . so too our lives are made. . . .
Richard Le Gallienne

Not something I can gather like a flower
Then lay aside to wither, nor can I
Prolong my life one instant past its hour.
Life is not my own to question or deny.
What then is life, this regal mystery —
Spirit and soul and sinew all in one?
This reaching out and up with an urgency
That stirs the heart and keeps the spirit young?
Our God of love gave us the gift of life;
Gave us bird and flower, sun and rain.
On journeys long or short, rebellion, strife,
As once in a garden we shall walk again —
Since at the heart's own center still we know
Love is the only rental that we owe.

A Newer Eden

I wonder if the ancient garden died

Of negligence with none to care, and none

To keep and dress the gift of beauty spun

In time's far dawn. Who loves will surely guide

Each seeking one to stepping stones inside

The wilderness. As love and truth are one

So falls the rain and shines the impartial sun

With both the gift and the Giver close beside.

I wonder, since the spirit never dies,

If those now gone can hear the music in the plume

Of willow boughs and know, when quickening clay

Wakes these kind hills, a newer Eden lies

In this small place — a song, one open bloom,

And someone waiting at the end of day.

Thanks be unto God for his unspeakable gift (2 Cor. 9:15).

Triolet for a Country Road

River road, leafy road, silver-green
  it winds
 Curving through the valleys and the high
   marsh grass
    Listening to the murmurs of the river
     it confines.
    River road, leafy road, silver-green
    it winds
   Through the hills and lowlands where its
    drowsy heart defines
  The whispers of the little towns beneath
   the overpass.
  River road, leafy road, silver-green
  it winds
 Curving through the valleys and the high
 marsh grass.

Thou visited the earth, and waterest it: thou
greatly enrichest it with the river of God,
which is full of water (Ps. 65:9).

Interim

He shall cover thee with his feathers,
and under his wings shalt thou trust:
his truth shall be thy shield and buckler
(Ps. 91:4).

Beyond the busy ways — I know
A place where, in the dawn,
Still-pools reflect a flowering land
Few have walked upon.

Almost as if a hand reached out,
Or voices called to me,
I know where lies the summer's gold,
The blue of sky and sea.

I know a place where a waterfall
Can all my thirsting slake;
Where wings, like praying hands, float by
On winds that do not break.

Any Time Now

This is the season of change —
New green on the burnished leaves of the oak.
The season of shine and glint on
Branches brittle and old. The season
When we look beyond a frostless window
Knowing that we, too, any time now and for
Our own special reasons, will be trimming
The rose tree, tying up the vine, learning
A new song to make our own world
Over again.

At times, Christians throughout the world of strife, turmoil, and the red-heat of war seek a place of quiet where they can be alone with the Lord in prayer. It is not always easy to find such a place, but it is a challenge to the best that is in the heart.

What better place to pour out the needs of body and soul than in the confines of a peaceful garden. There, through communion, our Lord reveals that His way is not just the best way but the only way to life everlasting.

And he hath put a new song in my mouth, even praise unto our God (Ps. 40:3).

Certainty

The sun is low, is high.
The tide comes in
and even the strongest wind
that rocks the island palms and rips the sails
cannot lower the level of the water.

I've watched
while the wind streams across the bay
pounding the shore, troubling the water —
the water level remains the same.

The tide goes out,
leaving its higher touch upon the sand;
but neither ocean waves nor thunder from the deep
can lift the water higher.

A man begins to see the unity of things.
And I, who lived beside the southern gulf
cannot keep from knowing
something more powerful than winds or hurricanes,
more quiet than the wings of the earth,
controls this ceaseless lift and fall;
this going out and coming in.

Blessed be the Lord God, the God of Israel, who only doeth wondrous things (Ps. 72:18).

This Then Is Love

Love is not a servant, not a master;

Love is not a whisper, not a dream,

Nor yet a simple keepsake laid away among

Life's souvenirs.

Love is not an asking, but a giving;

A sharing of the little and the much;

Crust, or honey and bread.

This then is love —

The perfect art of God that pours

Summer in the heart, warmer fires and

Brighter candlelight. Seldom

Understood, love understands.

When Past and Future Meet

Since this revolving world will change in part,
But not the longings of the human heart
Nor its fears,
I would ask of you who try to turn the page
Of curving silence back to lost light-years
And search the dust and ashes of our time.

How will you gauge the rhythm and the rhyme
Of centuries that shaped the meaning of our age?
I wonder if your searching hands will find
The small star-things we loved and left behind.
I wonder if a lover of the soil will know
A garden greened here in the fine spring rain,
Fruited, rested in the time of snow —
Then found its way to bloom in spring again.

When brittle winds have at last unfurled
An autograph of Love on old paths of the world
Then shall the vestige of a vanished age be
known.
Somewhere beneath immortal stars and skies
An older garden lies;
Its sure foundation stone
Still holds the canons for the first man and the
last.

So lies the past, with faith in each new day,
    The way a dove takes wing,
    The way the robins sing,
The way a garden knows the shining path
    That leads to spring.

That which hath been is now; and that
which is to be hath already been;
and God requireth that
which is past
(Eccles. 3:15).

Note from a Little Town

When curling yellow leaves come drifting down
In sobs of rain like fountain spray or tears,
I want to leave and find a little town
I have remembered all these rich, full years.

They dot the hills like shadows long and sweet —
A heritage of memories, soft refrains
Where all the country pathways know my feet.
Small towns change, but all that is whole remains.

I have come back where peace is a better thing
To see blue skies as leaves of forests part;
To listen to robins after-the-rain sing,
Attuned to the cool, quick lifting of the heart.

God loved small towns all hushed and starlight bright.
His Son was born in one that Holy Night.

*We have this hope
as an anchor for
our lives. It is safe
and sure* (Heb. 6:19;
Good News Bible).

Written and Signed

This place will never be abandoned now
For love has made of it
A new perfection. No fruit will fall,
No summer bough will stir,
No pathway point direction,
But I will think of you, who made it so.

When feather-songs lift wings
Across the blue; when homing footsteps
Autograph the snow to light my world,
I know that it is you.

Love is the glint of the plow;
The sowing and reaping; the vineyard
And the orchard gathered in;
Children waking and sleeping and
Dreaming of summertime or the white on white
Of a playtime hill.

And love is a lamp in the windy dark;
A thin-blue seam;
Clear windows to the day; the lyric,
The song, the sonnet, the note of love,
Written and signed.

He brought me to the
banqueting house, and his
banner over me was love
(Song of Sol. 2:4).

When the Harvest Is In

A farmer knows untended boundary lines
And barren fields can cost a man his bread.
The wild creeps in with shrub and forest-pine
And only token crops are harvested.

I think the land will never quite belong
To anyone. The earth, serene and proud
Sustains its own in silver tides of song
And wraps the sleeping in its emerald shroud.

May we (attending the Edens we think we own),
Tend well the garden of the heart's domain
Lest, like Dives, we give as alms — a stone
Instead of bread; store high the golden grain,
And hear all night a weeping at the sill
Where Lazarus lies alone, abandoned still.

Though I speak with the
tongues of men and of
angels, and have not charity,
I am become as sounding
brass, or a tinkling cymbal
(1 Cor. 13:1).

The Voice of the Mountains

(Glorieta)

I thought I heard a symphony

But the stillness was unbroken;

I thought I heard a sermon read,

Yet no word was spoken.

Voiced were the mystic mountains.

Though not a sound was heard

The shimmering, silver night revealed

God's music and His word.

Heaven and earth
shall pass away,
but my words
shall not
pass away
(Matt. 24:35).

Discovery

DOWN by the moss bank

Deep, so deep,

I found a bed of violets

Still half-asleep.

I SAW small petaled faces

With wonder looking up;

I saw bees drinking honey

From every dewy cup.

I FOUND a tiny open tomb

Deep beneath the sod;

I found far more than violets:

I found the pulse of God.

Unto thee it was shewed,
that thou mightest know that
the Lord he is God; there is none
else beside him (Deut. 4:35).

*W*inter Warmth

If I keep a green bough in my heart
a singing bird will come.

Old Chinese Proverb

On a night like this
When winter wraps us round, when window
Panes, immaculate as snow, are purified,
And Orion there in the East foretells
Months of winter-white,
How can we escape the winter
Of the heart?

Ye shall have a
song, as in the
night when a
holy solemnity
is kept; and
gladness of
heart (Isa.
30:29).

Winter's cloak
Reaches to the root,
And it is warm; winter's breath — the wood
That sings in the hearth, as once the
Wild birds sang on the green branch.
And now that a wreath of stars curves
About the dark — the cold of winter is
Powerless against the heart.

Closing Signature

Although the sun
Is further away and lower now —
Here and there a patch of green still clings
To the mountainside like a sampler
Spread across the southern slope.

Oh, sometimes I have seen this splendor
All the winter long; have seen it spread
Its way through fallen leaves
Of russet and gold, red, brown,
Pillowing fern and thyme where, earlier,
A young bird's singing told of spring, and,
Growing old — praised the summertime.

The season, too, grows old.
But like all things
Caught between the future and the past,
Summer leaves her mark: although
Folded now and still the wings
And the music of a song will be remembered;
The willow and the last golden leaf
Starring the brook; and in between
The brown and gold summer has signed her name.
How green her green.

Villanelle for Earth's Oldest Song

From sea to shore or some high leafy place
The wind and waves still sing earth's oldest song,
A melody that time cannot erase.

The whispering clock of time seems to trace
The music of David's harp — waves sing along
From sea to shore or some high leafy place.

The weeping and sighing of minor chords retrace
And bend the waves to a dirge, dying upon
A melody that time cannot erase.

Like sacred hymns that praise the Child of Grace
We hear the anthem's largo eastward on
From sea to shore or some high leafy place.

As breakers crash no current can replace
Or lose the song ten thousand voices strong
from sea to shore or some high place,
A melody that time cannot erase.

*But none saith,
Where is God my
maker, who giveth
songs in the night*
(Job 35:10).

Letter to a Child

Again and again I have followed this country road,
Always the same, to the river beyond the hill.
And yet today as I walked the current slowed,
Or seemed to slow, but my steps were slower still
As I listened to the far-off sound of wind and bird
Where earth's heart is warmer, the water colder.
I reach and feel the sweeping wind I heard
Caressing my hand. I notice, though time is older

It's about the way it was; there stand the same
Vine-covered bluffs and boulders that have been
Scarred by the years but anchored still. A name
On a rural box is changed, and now and then
An unfamiliar face. But the mornings sing
And the whispering rain at night still speaks of spring.

Prepared for change, only the dark seed changes,
Eventful, wind-sharp hours, a curving sweep
Of the shore, the weather. I recognize the ranges
Constant and sure; old pathways trodden deep —
Patterned with sun and shade where boughs, when shriven
Of leaves, still hold a star like a hand to hold.
The land replenishes all it has been given —
Sun and frost for the harvest, new yet old.

Feeling the force at their feet all who planted
Here planted well. The earth's sure increase,
Abundant, outstretched like golden wings, granted
Each need as it came, and a measure of peace.
When storms rage, when thunder shakes the sky,
I hear God's voice: *Peace, be still, it is I.*

Allow yourself to follow, if you can,
Time's blue curve. The earth will forever claim
Its rest, and higher shelves of rock still span
The shining clouds above the river. The same,
Yet not the same — men change — and now
That the stranger is friend I know his face,
His hand in mine; Strange how a name, somehow
When spoken aloud, becomes a part of a place.

This high, deep-rooted land is your legacy.
In coming back I have found enduring truth
Where all is music, peace, and serenity
(However peace is given) for age and youth.
Feel the power beneath this quickening loam.
Receive to your heart this place that I call home.

And now, brethren, I commend you to God, and to the word of his grace, which is able to build you up, and to give you an inheritance among all them which are sanctified (Acts 20:32).

Something
Somewhat like a rainbow, or a wing,
Something small,
Laid its bright reflection on the blue
And gold, or almost gold, surface
Of the stream.

Worship the Lord in the
beauty of holiness
(1 Chron. 16:29).

It could have been
A petal fallen from its stem; it might
Have been a leaf soaring on
An arc of wind,
Or the silken wings of a butterfly
Flushed from the willow withes whipped
By the autumn wind.

Whatever it was
(And I shall never know)
It brought meaning and beauty
To the green silences; it slowed my
Hurrying steps. As I trampled the wild
Grass I knew: vision, reflection,
Or dream, it was good
To be here.

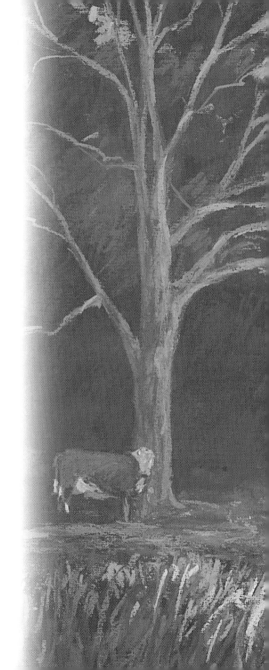

After the Storm

I have come here
to see this place that was my own —
now an alien land. Even the islands of
the gulf are new worlds of water and sand.
The eye of the hurricane,
gazing on the shore or the waves,
shaped a matrix of death. Yet, neither
life nor death is visible.

Only the sun is old,
the moon, stars, and the grotesque trees —
freed (now that the storm is gone), yet
bent to the earth as if still caged by
the wind as if there is nothing more,
not even this new rain-washed green like
the spill of spring that somehow roughed
the gale.

Even so,
a man who weathers his few short years,
changes, too.
But do not pity the step grown old —
touched by a thousand wonders that glance
and glint and linger. Pity the heart
grown old that has not planted deeper
furrows than ever the storm or years have
made, or has not reaped a
riper, richer grain.

For we walk by faith,
not by sight
(2 Cor. 5:7).

Second Sight

Although I cannot see
The tidal streams
That flow
Beneath the land
I see the honeyed grain
The harvest brings
Each autumn
From the fallow fields.

Although I cannot see
Your love, Love,
I know
It lies beneath
The simple daily tasks;
The lighted lamp
At dusk . . .
The glowing hearth.

The High Flock Passes

Surrendering to gardens overgrown,
Late summer covers the level meadowland
With riches all her own.
And tulip trees, still warm with summer sun,
Stand silver in the drenching rain, as though
They never bloomed at all.
Soon the autumn leaves, like yellow lace,
Will soften restless steps and hush the last
Sweet whisper in the garden.

So the hours drift, telling the way of fall
As the high flock leaves a shadow on the sun. . . .
So summer ends, song by song, petal by petal,
Leaf by golden leaf.

A golden glow is seen in the north;
and the glory of God fills us with awe
(Job 37:22; Good News Bible).

Letter to Our Children

Now that you have known this meadow
You will always know its song;
Now that you have known the mountain
You will always walk along
A forest trail of greenwood trees
Windward bent and set in stone;
The rainbow arch above the river
Will forever be your own.

These are more than rhyme and rhythm
Focusing upon the past;
They hold the cadence of the years
And set the stars steadfast.
When these are dimmed by stone and steel —
When the nights are overlong;
When you thirst, though fountains flow;
When listening, you hear no song.

Come, like a homing evening dove;
Come trudge the mountain trails you love.
Above the daisied meadow floor
You will hear the song once more.
Come, if you have need of these
And stand tall-measured by the trees.

Come ye children,
hearken unto me:
I will teach you the
fear of the Lord
(Ps. 34:11).

Autumn Twilight

How tranquil the garden, love, no sound at all
In the willow withes — autumn has come again.

The thread of music like a wild bird's call
Is silent now and a veil of warm thin rain
Falls low in the west, tangy and cool and sweet,
As though a newer Joshua empowers
This slant of sun that seems now to be
As moveless as the flowers.

Remember when, throughout the autumn days
We welcomed this pause before oncoming night?

Although I search for a newer, brighter phrase
Words cannot equate the quick delight
In a golden autumn leaf or a homing bird.
Something there is like a psalm or a gentle hand,
As though the Maker speaks and a sudden silence
Falls upon the land.

Autumn Song

Bird of sunlight and storm,
Friend of the weak and strong,
Both morning and evening
We listen for your song.
Bright as the changing sky
When the tempest breaks
Your song enchants the morning
And all the world awakes.
Light as one soft feather
On your downy breast,
Your gentle evening song
Lulls the world to rest.

*To every thing there is a season,
and a time to every purpose
under the heaven
(Eccles. 3:1).*

Wheat and Tares

Someone loved this meadow when spring
Showered the earth with bloom;
When leaves lay crimson at their feet,
When the yew was white.
Someone planted the fruit and vine;
Someone sowed the grain,
And lest their toil be spent in vain
Rested with the night
And called the labor good.
Someone harvested the wheat;
Someone burned the tares.
Then turning locks against the cold,
Bowed in prayer.

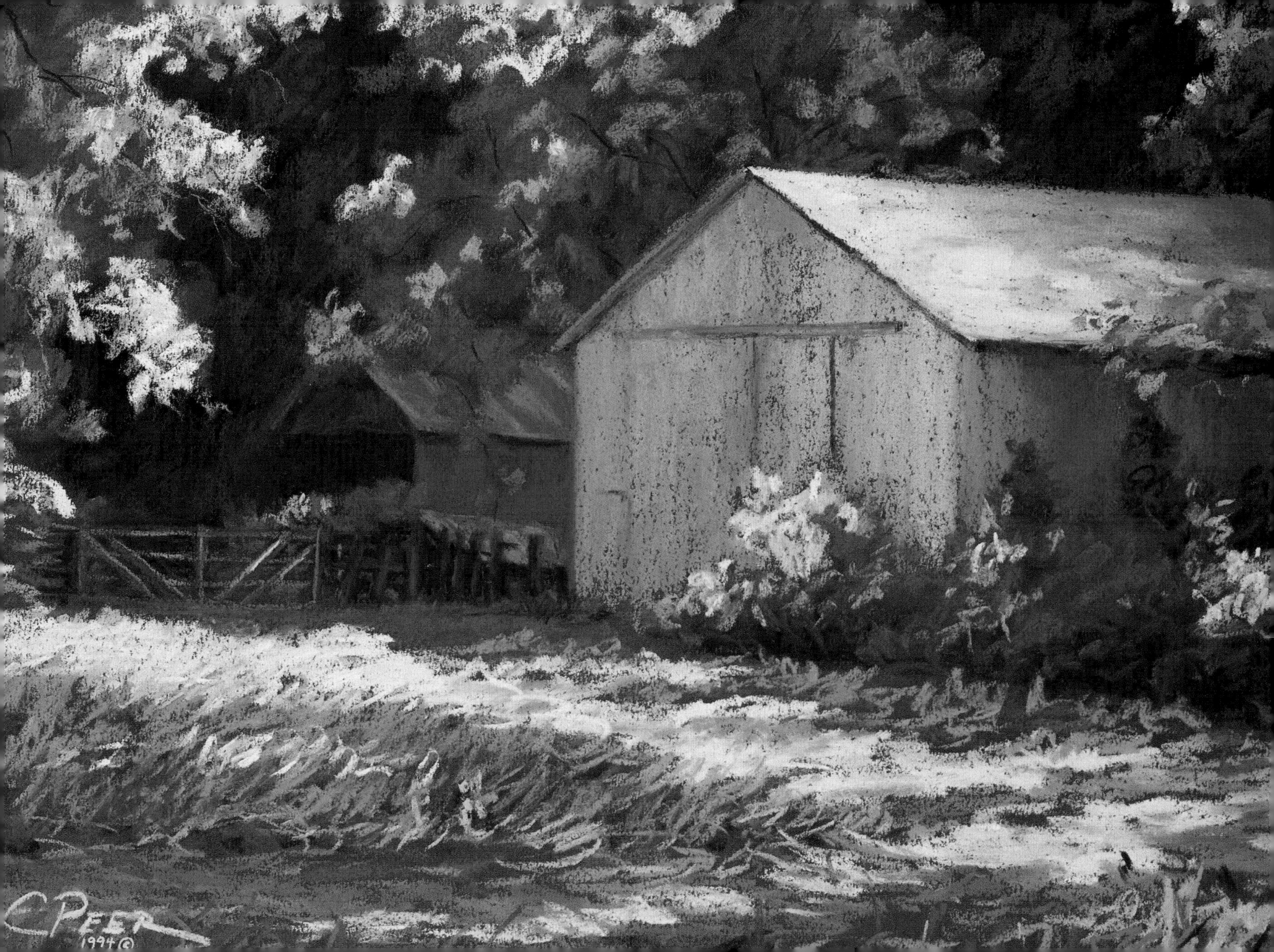
C PEER
1994©

hisper

Beside the mountain path
I watched a child lift a shell
(Bleached from the sun of centuries)
From grey outcropping stones
As old as time.

How small,
How young he looked, holding
A thousand, thousand years
In his hand.

In one magic moment
We looked upon the changeless
And the changed;
Marveled at the meeting here
Of old winds
And older tides;
Felt the salt-spray on our lips;
Heard the roar . . . low soughing . . .
And the silence
As the final wave
Left this whisper of an age
Buried in the dust.

But let him ask in faith, nothing
wavering. For he that wavereth
is like a wave of the sea driven
with the wind and tossed
(James 1:6).

With great appreciation
to the owners of these paintings.

Fall Wardrobe
North Arkansas Paper Company

Autumn Mirrored
The Bank of Fayetteville, N.A.

The Bend
The Bank of Fayetteville, N.A.

Evening Rays
The Bank of Fayetteville, N.A.

Shadows
The Bank of Fayetteville, N.A.

Nestled Beyond
The Bank of Fayetteville, N.A.

Rural Sunday
Karen Hutcheson and
Dave Wannemacher

Wanda's Arbor
Mr. and Mrs. Gene Hutto

Mrs. Pennington's Garden
Mrs. Cecilia Peer

Our Common Path
Dr. and Mrs. Marvin Mumme

Pool of Color
Mr. and Mrs. Ralph Irwin

Blueberry Creek
Mr. James D. Garner

Redbuds in the Valley
Dr. and Mrs. Scott Stinnett

Phlox and Hollyhocks
Mr. and Mrs. Jim Robason

Orvie's Way
Mr. and Mrs. David Whitt

Morning Shadows
Mr. and Mrs. David Whitt

Aunt Buffa's
Mr. and Mrs. Roger Burkett

Gold Ridge
Mr. and Mrs. Bill Hutcheson

Reflected Colors
Mr. and Mrs. Sandy Sanders

Through the Light
Mr. and Mrs. John Horn

Maggie's Gate
Mr. and Mrs. Jon Olmstead

Corner Post
Ms. Jennifer Parks (Cover)

Lighting the Way
Mr. and Mrs. Harry Keifer

September Warmth
Dr. and Mrs. Robert V. Borg

Summer Field
Mr. and Mrs. Fred Stuckey

Trees Ablaze
Mr. and Mrs. Fred Stuckey

Beside Still Waters
Rogers Clinic for Women

Going Home
North Arkansas Paper Company

Charles E. Peer grew up in Van Buren, Arkansas, where he received his first formal art training at the age of 12. He received a bachelor's degree from Hendrix College in Conway, Arkansas, and began graduate studies at the University of Denver, Colorado. Mr. Peer received his Master of Fine Arts degree from the University of Arkansas in Fayetteville, Arkansas, in 1979.

Mr. Peer established his studio/gallery in the Historic District of Van Buren, Arkansas, in 1980. In 1990 he and his family relocated to Siloam Springs, Arkansas, where he heads the Department of Art and Design at John Brown University.

Along with his teaching responsibilities, Mr. Peer continues to display his work in one-man and group exhibits and to lead workshops throughout the region. Mr. Peer's paintings, which have received recognition in many exhibits and competitions, are currently represented in several galleries across Arkansas, found in many corporate and private collections, and been used as illustrations by DaySpring Greeting Cards of Siloam Springs, Arkansas.

Charles and his wife, Cecilia, have been married since 1984 and have one daughter, Jordan.

May Harris Gray was born in Canton, Kentucky, and was educated in Kentucky, Illinois, and Louisiana. After receiving a teacher's certificate she taught school and music in Louisiana before her marriage to Thomas Virgil Gray (now deceased). They had three children: Jean Peer, Dorothy Edwards (deceased), and Thomas Virgil Gray, Jr.

She is a Life Member of the Poetry Society of America, a member of the National League of American Pen Women, the Kentucky State Poetry Society, and the Poet's Roundtable of Arkansas. She was co-founder of the Fort Smith Branch, the first of many branches of the Poet's Roundtable of Arkansas. This organization named her "Poet of the Present" and presented her the C.C. Allard Gold Cup as "Poet of the Year."

The poetry of May Harris Gray has been published in magazines, literary quarterlies, church literature, newspapers, and anthologies: "Our Christian Home and Family" published by Harper and Row, "Kentucky in American Letters," "Poets of the Midwest," and the "Poets' Roundtable Anthology," among others. She has judged poems for state competitions in several states and is listed in Marquis' "Who's Who of American Women," "Arkansas Lives," and "Who's Who in Poetry, England."